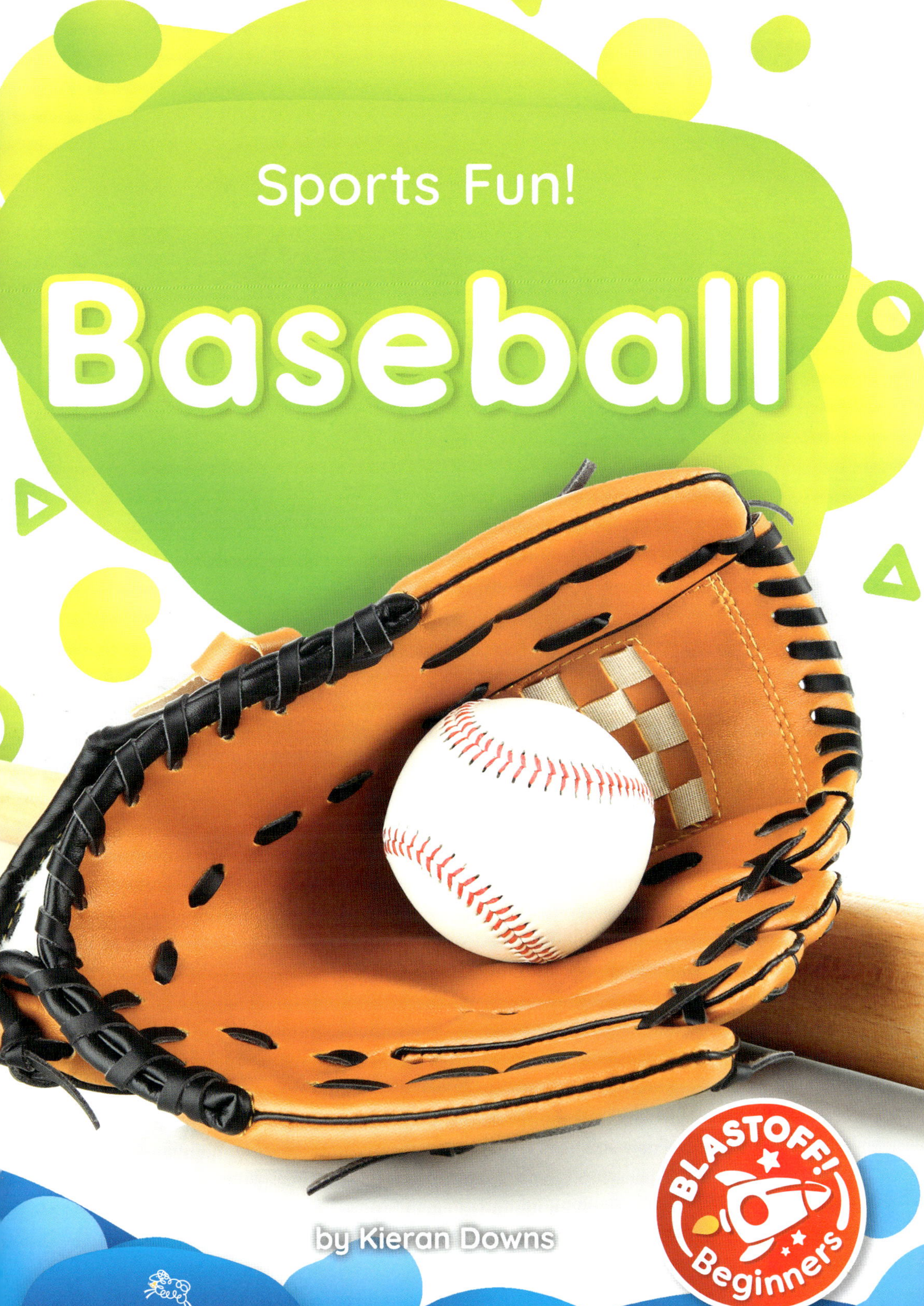
Sports Fun!
Baseball
by Kieran Downs
BLASTOFF! Beginners
BELLWETHER MEDIA
MINNEAPOLIS, MN

Blastoff! Beginners are developed by literacy experts and educators to meet the needs of early readers. These engaging informational texts support young children as they begin reading about their world. Through simple language and high frequency words paired with crisp, colorful photos, Blastoff! Beginners launch young readers into the universe of independent reading.

Sight Words in This Book

a	is	other	they	we
first	it	our	this	
get	more	out	three	
has	now	play	time	
have	on	run	to	
he	one	the	two	

This edition first published in 2024 by Bellwether Media, Inc.

Library of Congress Cataloging-in-Publication Data

Names: Downs, Kieran, author.
Title: Baseball / by Kieran Downs.
Description: Minneapolis, MN : Bellwether Media, Inc., 2024. | Series: Blastoff! Beginners : Sports fun! | Includes bibliographical references and index. | Audience: Ages 4-7 | Audience: Grades K-1
Identifiers: LCCN 2023004974 (print) | LCCN 2023004975 (ebook) | ISBN 9798886873900 (library binding) | ISBN 9798886875782 (ebook)
Subjects: LCSH: Baseball--Juvenile literature.
Classification: LCC GV867.5 .D72 2024 (print) | LCC GV867.5 (ebook) | DDC 796.357--dc23/eng/20230202
LC record available at https://lccn.loc.gov/2023004974
LC ebook record available at https://lccn.loc.gov/2023004975

Editor: Rebecca Sabelko Designer: Jeffrey Kollock

Printed in the United States of America, North Mankato, MN.

Table of Contents

Game Time!

We get
our gloves.
It is time
to play baseball!

What Is Baseball?

Baseball is a team sport. Teams have nine players.

team

Two teams play on a **field**. They try to get **runs**.

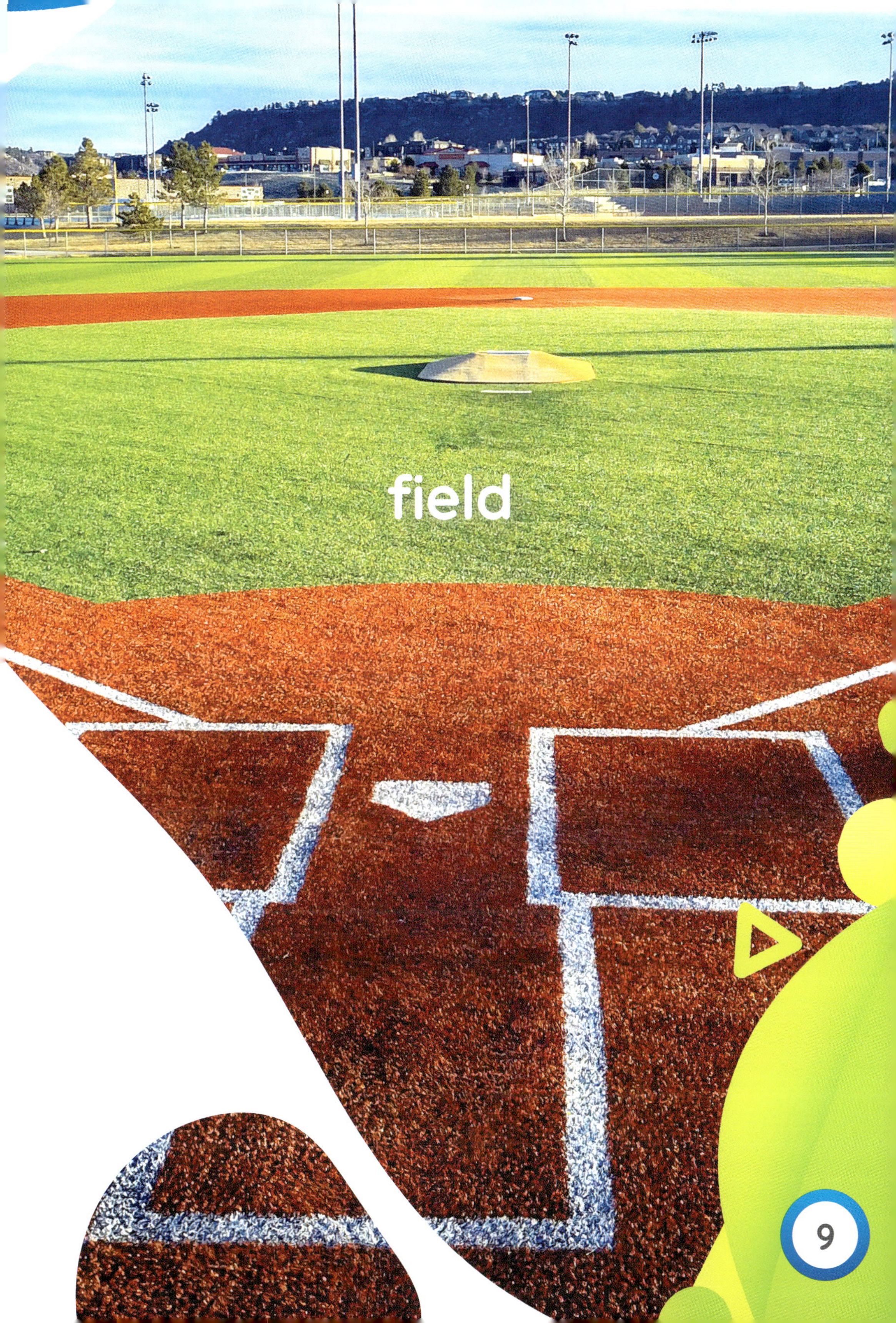
field

On the Field

One team bats first. They try to hit the ball.

batting

The other team throws. They catch hit balls.

throwing

They try to get three **outs**.

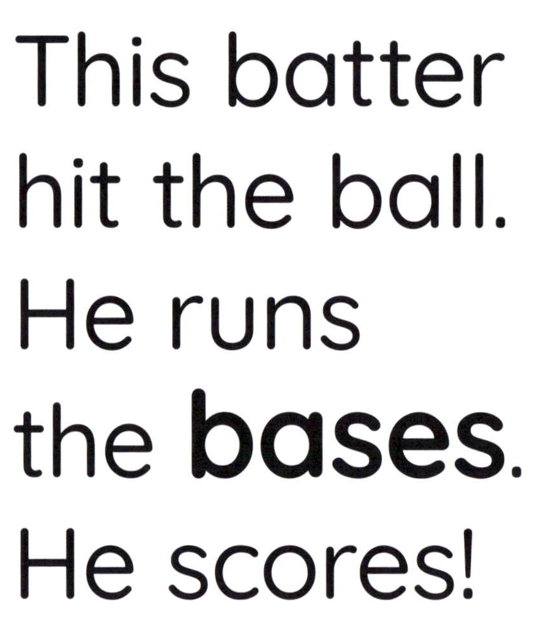

This batter
hit the ball.
He runs
the **bases**.
He scores!

base

The next batter is out. Now the teams trade sides.

The game is over.
This team has
more runs.
They win!

Baseball Facts

Playing Baseball

Baseball Moves

hit the ball

catch the ball

run the bases

Glossary

bases

parts of a baseball field where runners stand

field

a place where baseball games are played

outs

when players at bat or runners must leave the field

runs

points scored in baseball

To Learn More

ON THE WEB

FACTSURFER

Factsurfer.com gives you a safe, fun way to find more information.

1. Go to www.factsurfer.com.
2. Enter "baseball" into the search box and click 🔍.
3. Select your book cover to see a list of related content.

Index

The images in this book are reproduced through the courtesy of: Africa Studio, front cover; Ronnie Chua, pp. 3 (glove), 20; GMessina, p. 4; RonTech2000, p. 5; KPG-Payless, pp. 7, 22 (catch); Phillip Rubino, p. 9; tammykayphoto, pp. 11, 13, 22 (hit), 23 (runs); Lopolo, p. 15; John Konrad, p. 16; jpbcpa, p. 17; RBFried, p. 19; Ariel Skelley/ Getty Images, p. 21; mTaira, p. 22 (playing baseball); JoeSAPhotos, p. 22 (run); Dan Thornberg, p. 23 (bases); Brian Karczewski, p. 23 (field); sirtravelalot, p. 23 (outs).